SCENES FOR YOUNG PERFORMERS TO ENJOY

by

To Lily – Hope you enjoy performing these!

ELEANOR McLEOD

Eleanor McLeod

CheckPoint
Press

Scenes For Young Performers To Enjoy! Vol I Monologues
ISBN-13: 978-1-906628-41-3
Published by CheckPoint Press, Ireland

www.checkpointpress.com

CheckPoint Press
Books for Training and Education

Other books by this author from CheckPoint Press
ISBN: 978-1-906628-23-9 Poems for Children to Enjoy
ISBN: 978-1-906628-19-2 More Poems for Children to Enjoy
ISBN: 978-1-906628-46-8 Scenes for Young Performers to Enjoy (II)

INTRODUCTION

As a teacher and also an examiner and adjudicator in the exciting realm of Speech and Drama, I am all too aware of how difficult it is to find original and appealing scenes for young performers. This collection of scenes is based on characters from familiar fairy stories, many by Hans Anderson and The Brothers Grimm, in which I have taken a different slant, often to modernise them. So, we have the Mother Bear who is all too aware of compensation culture or Red Riding Hood's Grandma being hounded by the press! Others are more traditional. All of them have already been performed by keen young actors and actresses so that I have been able to see how they translate into performances.

I do hope that you will enjoy performing them.

Eleanor McLeod

Table of Contents

*   *   *

1

THE PRINCESS AND THE PEA

☦

"The Princess and the Pea" is one of Hans Anderson's shortest stories, but the character of the Queen who wants to make sure that her son marries a real Princess is surely a familiar one! Even in the few lines in which she is described we see what a forceful character she must have been – and that is what I hope comes out in this speech in a humorous way. I like the way the original story ends with this one sentence: "There, that is a true story." Perhaps Hans Anderson was writing about a mother-in-law he actually knew!

*   *   *

THE PRINCESS AND THE PEA

QUEEN: What impertinence! To think that she could pass herself off as a princess! She's got her eye on our son, Prince Bertie you know, and she thinks that she can come here with her hoity-toity ways and fool us. Well, we've seen enough princesses to know that she isn't one, haven't we my dear? Remember that scullery maid who stole all my jewels and my best gown and pretended that she was the heiress to the throne of Kitchenalia! I spotted her immediately, didn't I dear? Yes, I know she was wearing my things, but it wasn't that obvious. I'm not stupid you know. What did you say? I'll pretend I didn't hear that. Well, this time I have set her the ultimate test. Test dear, not vest. Oh I am so glad that Bertie seems to be following me rather his father or I would feel sorry for any girl that got him – Princess or not. Anyway, I have placed a very small pea under the twelve mattresses on her bed. Yes, twelve mattresses. How did she get on top of them? Well I got her a stepladder of course – don't make things difficult dear. Sometimes I wonder why I married you. What? You were a King, yes, well that's beside the point. Even Kings can have their drawbacks. Where was I? Yes, now, only a Princess will be able to feel a teensy weensy pea under the thickness of twelve mattresses. It is the test that cannot fail. No, it's a dried pea, not a cooked pea, she won't have squashed it – really, sometimes you can be very dim. Those jewels in your crown are the only bright thing about you sometimes. I don't think you care, do you? You'd see our son marry some jumped up little madam who'd throw us out of our palace the moment she smelt the crown. Ah, here she comes. Now we'll find out. And don't you be too nice. Good morning, how did you sleep *princess?* You didn't? *(whispering to the king)* She didn't sleep very well. (*To the Princess*) Why was that? A lump under the mattress! But that's impossible, they were the finest duckdown, soft as a marshmallow, smooth as…. You found a what? A pea. How strange. Look at this dear, it's a pea. Now tell me Princess, have you met our son, Prince Bertie…I'm sure that he would love to meet you.

*   *   *

2

THE FROG PRINCE

✝

The Story of the Frog Prince is a very familiar one and indeed the modern witticism that you have to kiss a lot of frogs before you find your prince is just one of the legacies of this story. It was written by the Brothers Grimm whose stories could be quite dark and gruesome as they were written for adults as well as children. In fact, in the original story the Princess is never asked to kiss the frog and it's only when she picks him up and throws him against the wall that he turns into a prince! This made me wonder what sort of bad tempered bride this poor prince was getting, and so this rather plaintive monologue came about. I hope you feel a bit sorry for him too!

*   *   *

THE FROG PRINCE

PRINCE: It had its advantages being a frog you know. Not many, but there are times when I quite fancy being back in that well. Most fairy stories end with "and they lived happily ever after", don't they, but this one didn't you see. Oh, she's beautiful enough. I knew as soon as I saw her that she was the most beautiful princess who was likely to come along to the well that day – there weren't many around at the time of course. She promised me she'd do anything if I got her golden ball back and I believed her. I should have known then that she was going to be trouble. Did she keep her word? No, she did not. I had to follow her all the way to the palace and that's quite a long hop I can tell you. I gave her the little poem I'd practised, I thought it was quite good, plenty of pathos and appeal:

King's daughter, King's daughter, open for me;
You promised that I your companion should be,
When you sat in the shade from the sun's bright
beam,
And I fetched up your ball from the fountain's
cool stream.

Alright, it's not Wordsworth, I'll give you that, but I thought it might do the trick?

Not on your nelly!

"I don't want any warty, ugly old frog in my room", she said. That hurt me that did. I thought that for a frog

I was quite good looking. She kept up quite a song and dance about me, temper tantrums, tears, the lot, went on for days. I thought she'd have exhausted herself with all the histrionics, but she could keep going…and going. And if anything it just got louder. I should have gone back to the well then really, at least it would have been quiet. Anyway, her father told her that she had to keep her word and so very reluctantly, she agreed, but I could see that she really didn't want me around at all, I mean picking you up and throwing you against the wall isn't exactly showing affection is it? The kiss only came about when I hopped on her pillow while she was sleeping. She was suitably impressed when I changed back into myself of course and as she had no better offers her father said she ought to marry me, but once a bad tempered little minx always a….heigh ho, does anybody know of a witch living roundabout that changes Princes into frogs?

*   *   *

3

RAPUNZEL

✝

"Rapunzel" is another story by the Brothers Grimm. So many so called 'fairy' stories are actually about witches and when the brothers were writing their stories in the early part of the nineteenth century people still had a belief in the folklore of witches and evil influences. In this story a man and his wife give away their only daughter to a witch in exchange for a few lettuces – not a good swap really! Of course, Rapunzel grows up to be extremely beautiful with the obligatory long blonde hair and then – enter a handsome prince. It's the stuff of which all good fairy stories are made. The witch of course, is, as we expect, wicked with 'cruel and malicious eyes', but another requirement of a good fairy story is that they live happily ever after and even though the prince escapes from the witch he is blinded by thorns as he jumps from the tower, but eventually finds Rapunzel again and she cures him and they do, as the story says, spend their days 'in happiness and content'. I hope you enjoy playing this nasty old witch.

*   *   *

RAPUNZEL

WITCH: Rapunzel, Rapunzel, let down your hair
That I may climb without a stair.

Thank you my dear. *(She mimes climbing up the hair.)* Well, what have you been doing today, spinning, weaving, painting? Singing?! Singing what? You don't know any songs, you have never even heard any music. Come here, come into the light, let me look at your face. You have roses in your cheeks where usually you are as pale as a lily. And your eyes are sparkling where they are usually lifeless and sad. Something has happened here today. Something that has changed you from a sad, miserable, pale child into a beautiful young woman. Tell me. You will tell me, you wicked child. What do I hear you say? The King's son! I thought I had hidden you from all the world in this dark tower, but somehow you have managed to betray me. You will pay dearly for this. How did he find you this King's son? Did you send signals to him? I knew I should have blocked up these windows. Wait, I remember now, I thought I saw someone hiding among the trees the other day, there was a shadow, a movement, but I believed it to be the wind in the leaves. He must have overheard me. So he discovered our secret. Well I'll put a stop to that little game. I'll cut off your hair this instant. I have the shears here. Don't struggle, you know how strong I am and you are like a reed in the wind. You stand no chance against the strength of my powers. This won't take long. He will never be able to reach you again. *(She cuts*

16

*Rapunzel's hair.)*Keep still you wretched creature. There, that's done. I have always wanted to have beautiful golden hair like this. Would it suit me do you think? Wait, I think I hear your Prince, well he's about to get a big surprise. *(She holds the hair out of the window)*. Ah, you are come to fetch your loving bride I suppose, but to you Rapunzel is lost forever. The beautiful bird has had her feathers plucked and will never sing again. Now leave this tower and forget that you ever saw her. And I hope you've got a good head for heights, because you're going to have to jump!

*   *   *

4

LITTLE RED
RIDING HOOD

✝

Here is another rather frightening story by the Brothers Grimm, but this time the nasty character is a big bad wolf. We all know that he eats up the grandmother and in the original story he also eats Red Riding Hood! So, how does the story end? All good fairy stories should have a happy ending and the baddie should get his come-uppance. Well, I'm happy to relate that by the wonders of the power of the storyteller, both Grandmother and Red Riding Hood are rescued by a hunter who fortunately happens to be passing by and kills the wolf and finds the two ladies still alive inside! Indeed, in one line we are told that she could scarcely breathe as she came out of his stomach, but a few lines later she, "drank the wine and ate the cake" which Red Riding Hood had brought! This suggested to me that this granny was no ordinary lady – there is another incident tagged on to the end of the original story that tells us how she foiled another wolf in his attempt to eat them, so I hope you agree with me that when you play her you find that she is quite a character! I have imagined her talking to the press who have come around to report the story.

*   *   *

LITTLE RED RIDING HOOD

GRANDMA: You want to interview me? Well of course, I'd be delighted. Would you like me sit here? Oh my goodness, this is so exciting, I feel like a film star. Yes, I am Red Riding Hood's Grandmother. I don't look old enough to be a grandmother! Oh you are a flatterer young man. Now what do you want to know? Well, yes it was a very traumatic day I can tell you. It all began in the morning. You see, because it was a Monday I was doing my washing. I always do my washing on a Monday. My mother did her washing on a Monday and so I've always done the same. I take great pride in my washing you know, spotless it is. What's that? Oh I'm sorry, yes I'll get on with it. Well I went outside to peg my washing on the line. There was a lovely breeze blowing and if you get the washing out early then it's dry by lunchtime and you can iron it. I don't like ironing as much as I like washing, but…. Yes, yes, of course I'll get on to the Wolf. Well, I heard a rustle in the bushes behind me, just over here. This is a blackcurrant bush you know, gives me delicious blackcurrants and I make the most beautiful jam, I'll have to give you a jar. The best ones are over here because they get the most sun. Big and plump and juicy they are….You want me to what? Oh, stay in front of the camera. I'm sorry. Now this rustling turned out to be the Wolf. Oh yes, very big he was, with wicked eyes and huge sharp teeth and he chased me into the house. I can't run very fast because I've got a bit of arthritis in this knee. It's alright some days but if there's a bit of damp in the air then it's very painful. Alright, alright, I'm coming to the good bit. Yes he did! He locked me in the cupboard and stole my nightie off the line. Not quite dry it wasn't. He'll be having arthritis if he's not careful and serve him right I say. You have to make sure that things are aired you see or….Anyway, to cut a long story short, Red Riding Hood came in, didn't know it was the Wolf, he was about to eat her and I leapt out of the cupboard, hit him over the head with my walking stick and threw him in the washing tub. I was about to put him through the mangle when he decided he'd had enough and ran off and we haven't seen him since. What? No, all in a day's work dear. It was Monday you see, washing day.

*   *   *

5

SLEEPING BEAUTY

✝

66"The Sleeping Beauty in the Wood" is the full title of this story by the Brothers Grimm. It has always seemed to me to be one of the most magical of fairy tales with its good and bad fairies and then the spell cast on everyone to send them to sleep for a hundred years. A more modern audience would find this a little difficult to come to terms with I think and when you consider what has happened to our world in the last 100 years and how things have changed, that is hardly surprising – so that was the inspiration for this next scene.

*　　*　　*

THE SLEEPING BEAUTY

COOK: *(Waking up and looking around)* Ooh, I'm so stiff. I must have dropped off. Eeugh! What's this on my face, cobwebs! Cobwebs in my kitchen, I won't have that. Oh, oh, my leg's gone to sleep *(Hops around)* Just look at the mess in here – and the smell! That bread's gone quite mouldy and that pudding is green. What's in this saucepan. Yuch! It stinks. The fire's cold. The shelves are covered with dust and this floor is thick with leaves and dead mice and beetles. Oh dear, oh dear, I've never seen anything like it in my life. I must have been asleep for a lot longer than I thought. Let's have a look through the window. If I can look through that is; it's absolutely filthy – and there's ivy growing through it and ouch! brambles. That gardener hasn't been doing what he's paid for. What on earth is that? It looks like a funny sort of carriage but there's smoke coming out of the back of it and it's making a very peculiar noise. Hello, there's somebody at the back door. *(Opens door)* Yes, I am the palace cook. You've brought me what? A refrigerator? What on earth is a refrigerator. It keeps things cold! Listen, this palace is quite cold enough as it is, even with the fire going full blast it can still be freezing in here. A freezer? You've brought one of those as well? Look, I told you, it's freezing enough without....central heating...what's central heating? Oh, I see. The new Prince has asked for it to be installed. I didn't know we had a new Prince. And who might you be young man, coming in here with all your fancy notions and gadgets? You've been sent by the new young Princess to bring the palace kitchens up to date! But the last time I saw her she had just had a very sad accident and... You're an electrician, I see, well what's an electrician when he's at home? Can you, can you indeed? So if I just go over there and flick this little thing – oh my goodness, where did that light come from. Can I try it again? It's wonderful. Off. On. Off. On. Look at that! Why haven't I seen one of these before? Asleep? Yes, I know I dropped off a little while ago, but I'd been working very hard and the tiredness just came over me all of a sudden and....it wasn't a little while ago? It was how long ago? A hundred years! But, but, I don't look any different do I? I don't look old do I? Thank goodness for that. There's something to be said for magic. His Highness the Prince has ordered that the palace be rewired and replumbed as soon as possible! Well, you'd better carry on then – and I'd better start cleaning this place up. You can put the fridge over there. And can I just try that switch again?

*   *   *

6

SNOW WHITE AND THE SEVEN DWARFS (I)

✝

❝Snow White and the Seven Dwarfs" must be one of the most popular of Grimm's fairy tales and of course it is still going strong in pantomime every Christmas. This tale has at its heart the victory of good over evil and the longed for happy ending with the Prince and Snow White living happily ever after. What I liked about the Disney version was that the dwarfs took on distinct personalities too. In this monologue I've considered a moment in the story which maybe hasn't had the most focus in dramatic representations. You can choose to be any one of the dwarfs as they think that Snow White is dead.

*   *   *

SNOW WHITE AND THE SEVEN DWARFS (i)

DWARF: Come along my brothers, our dinner will be getting cold and Snow White will be cross if the food is spoiled. I'm really hungry tonight. I hope it's a lovely stew. Snow White makes a most delicious stew. Stop! Remember to take your boots off and put your tools in the shed. Now that our house is so lovely and clean we don't want to mess it up. *(He opens the door)* Snow White, we're home! I love it when she says, "Did you have a good day my dears?" even if it wasn't a good day it always seems like one when we see her smile. The house always smells warm and cosy now. Our slippers are laid out by the fire and the cushions are plumped up on our chairs and there is always something ready for our supper. Snow White! Where can she be? Wait a minute, what's that over there, just under the table; it looks like her shoes. It is her shoes, but her feet are still in them. Snow White, are you alright? She can't be asleep, not here on the floor. What's this? She has a strange necklace around her neck and it's made a horrible mark as if it's much too tight. I'll take it off. And what's that glinting in her hair? It's a strange sort of comb, but it seems to be glowing. *(He puts out his hand to touch it)* Ow! This is no ordinary comb, I think it's poisoned. Quickly, quickly, get some water or some medicine or something to revive her. Who could have done this? It must have been the wicked Queen, but how did she get in here? We told Snow White to let no-one in, to keep the door firmly locked. She must have put her into a deep sleep or worse. That woman is evil and her one wish was to see Snow White dead. Snow White, Snow White, please wake up. Is she still breathing? My brothers, I can't feel any breath, any pulse. I think that our beloved Snow White must be dead. She looks so beautiful still with her skin so pale, her lips so red and her hair of ebony. How will we live without her? We will make her a glass coffin and place it on the mountain side so that we can still look at her each day as we go off to work. This is the saddest day of our lives.

*　　*　　*

7

SNOW WHITE AND THE SEVEN DWARFS (II)

T he other character that is most intriguing in "Snow White" is the Wicked Queen – a part that any character actress would love to play.

In this scene I have created a reason for her wanting to be the most beautiful woman in the world!

*   *   *

SNOW WHITE AND THE SEVEN DWARFS (ii)

WICKED QUEEN: *(Entering with a dramatic flourish)* Well hello everybody, I'm here! I don't think you need to look any further for your Miss World. Why not save all the expense of a lavish show and just crown me now. Why am I so sure? Who are you dear and what do you know about beautiful women – don't answer that, we haven't got time to waste. Well you see, I have a magic mirror and it is able to see all the women in the world and then report back to me who is the most beautiful and every time I have asked it – well, apart from a little hiccup a while ago – every time it has told me that I am the most beautiful. What was the little hiccup? Oh some poor girl who was very lovely, but alas, *(she takes out her handkerchief)* she had a most unfortunate accident. *(She pretends to weep)* I'm sorry, it does so upset me when I think of her, I have such a tender heart you see. I want peace and love for everyone all over the world, that is my sincere wish. What talents do I have? Well, I'm a very accomplished actress. Why, sometimes, to amuse my friends I dress up as an old witch and they tell me I'm really convincing. *(She throws her scarf over her head and becomes the witch)* Have I got anything that you would like to buy, my dear? What about this pretty necklace? Yes, of course you can try it on. Because it's poisoned, you stupid little girl! *(Coming out of character)* Oh, sorry, I got a bit carried away there. Good though, aren't I? My figure is superb. My skin is as soft as satin and I never seem to age. I could go on being Miss World for years. And I have a very powerful effect on men. They do anything I say. See that one in the audience there, that handsome huntsman who is shaking in his boots. You would do anything I asked wouldn't you? WOULDN'T YOU! There we are you see. Of course he does work for me so he couldn't really disagree. So what are you waiting for? Do you want me as Miss World or not? I look wonderful in a swimsuit, I have enough money to pay off any of the other pathetic little candidates and I could make life very difficult for all of you. What's that? My mirror! Who has brought that here? How dare you? It says what?! It's a fake! It's a fraud! *(She takes off her shoe and throws it at the mirror)* That's what I think of you, you stupid thing. Now where's that huntsman gone. Come here you, you've got some very serious questions to answer. Where are you!

*   *   *

8

THUMBELINA

✝

W e are back to Hans Anderson with our next story, "Thumbelina". I expect, like me, you know that the central character is a very tiny little girl, but it wasn't until I came to read the story again that I realised that there are lots of interesting characters in the story too. She is rescued by a kindly fieldmouse, but the nature of the story takes on quite a sinister feel as we realise that he is trying to marry Tiny – the name given to her in this part of the story – to his friend Mr Mole, who would then take her to live with him under the ground and she would never see the light of day again. Fortunately she escapes this fate with the help of a friendly swallow, leaving Mr Fieldmouse to share his thoughts.

*   *   *

THUMBELINA

FIELD MOUSE: I couldn't believe it! I just couldn't believe it. She went – just like that! After all that I had done for her. I took her in you know when she was nearly starving and freezing to death. I heard a tap on this door and I opened it and there she was, trembling and blue.

"May I have a small piece of barleycorn, for I haven't eaten for days, " she begged.

Well I couldn't say no could I? I'm not that sort of chap. So I brought her in and put her to sit over there and made her a hot drink and she stayed with me – all through the winter. I didn't really mind having an extra mouth to feed because she helped with the housework. When I say helped, I mean she did most of it. Well she offered and I didn't want to dampen her enthusiasm, I'm not that sort of chap. But that's what gave me the idea of suggesting her as a wife for my good friend Mole. He's got a very big house you see and he does find it a bit hard to keep it spick and span on account of the fact that he's a bit short sighted. Of course I didn't tell her that when I suggested him as a husband. I made him sound rather attractive – well off, wears a beautiful black velvet coat, very rich and learned, own house and good sense of humour. I made that bit up, but I have made him laugh once or twice and when I told him about Thumbelina, he smiled.

He took an instant fancy to her of course. Well she was very pretty – but he couldn't really see that. It was the songs she sung about the flowers and the sunshine that he liked, because he's never really been a fan of the great outdoors; he prefers his underground tunnels. Anyway, he asked her to marry him. I had to prompt him you know because he's very shy and I'm sure she nodded, so I began to make all the arrangements, I like to be helpful, I'm that sort of chap. The wedding clothes were of wool and linen for she could have only the best as the Mole's wife. Then out of the blue she turns to me and she says:

"I won't marry that disagreeable Mole. I won't!

"What nonsense!" I told her, "He's very handsome and very rich, so don't you be so obstinate after all I've done for you." I could have been even crosser but I'm not that sort of chap.

"I won't be shut away under the ground and not see the sunshine and the blue skies again" she cried. I tried to reason with her but all she did was burst into tears and run out into the cornfield. And that's the last we saw of her. I wouldn't be surprised that she came to a bad end, probably eaten by a weasel or a fox. Such a pity. She could have had all she wanted. Women, I just don't understand them. They're not like us chaps.

* * *

9

THE
WILD SWANS

✝

The story of the Wild Swans is not as well known as some of Hans Anderson's other stories, but it is a very beautiful one and like so many other tales has at its centre a wicked stepmother and a princess, Eliza who is not only beautiful but also "too good and too innocent for witchcraft to have any power over her." Her eleven brothers have been turned into swans and she, not knowing this, sets out to look for them. In this scene she finds them again, but discovers that they can only be human until dawn and then they will change back into swans again. It is Eliza's brave and determined efforts, in which she has to endure much pain and is eventually condemned to death for being a witch, that finally conquer the evil of the spell and, thankfully, she is rescued at the last moment and goodness and virtue win the day. I think it is one of the loveliest of his stories.

*   *   *

THE WILD SWANS

ELIZA: *(Waking up)* Where am I? Oh yes, now I remember, I'm in the wood. I must have fallen asleep. Did I see angels up there last night, or was it as the old woman said, some beautiful white swans? I must carry on, however tired I am and find my brothers. Perhaps if I follow this river it will take me out of the wood – it seems to be lighter over there and I can see blue sky. At the end of this path there might be... *(She stops in amazement)*...can I believe my eyes? Is that the sea? It must be, for the ground under my feet is becoming sandy and the stones here are not coarse and sharp like they were in the wood, they are smooth, as smooth as glass. How lovely this pebble is, its colours are all the brighter because it's so smooth. The waves roll on without getting weary and they make everything beautiful. Thank you for that lesson waves, for now I know that if I carry on, the way will become smoother and easier and I will find my brothers again. There's some seaweed over there and something white shining on top of it, I wonder what it can be. *(She moves over to the seaweed)* They are feathers, white feathers and there are...one, two *(she counts)*...eleven of them...just the same number as my brothers. How lovely they are. I will keep them safe, for the wind is getting up and the waves are looking angry and night is coming on and the feathers might blow away. *(She looks up)* What is that? There's something in the sky coming out of the far horizon. Something is flying this way, it looks like a big bird – there are more of them, lots of white birds, with big, beautiful wings and long graceful necks. They look like swans and they are coming to land on this beach. I'll hide behind this dune and watch so that I don't frighten them away. What are they doing? Their feathers seem to be falling off and they are changing shape. It's my brothers, my dearest brothers. *(Running out)* I'm here! I'm here! It's me, it's Eliza! Oh my brothers, I've been looking everywhere for you. What happened to you? Enchanted? By our wicked stepmother! And you can only stay as yourselves until dawn? Oh how I hate her and what she has done to you. Can I break the spell? What can I do to help you? No, don't change back again, don't turn into swans again. Don't fly away.Take me with you, please take me with you.

*   *   *

10

THE
SNOW QUEEN

✝

The character of the evil Snow Queen who spears the heart of Kay and puts him under her spell is not so different from the White Witch in the Narnia books and Hans Anderson's story is long and complex. This scene is from the beginning of the story when Kay is first struck by the icicles and immediately his personality begins to change and his sister Gerda and his grandmother are the first to experience this. The rest of the story follows Gerda on her journey to find Kay and bring him back. It is his sister's hot tears that eventually thaw the lump of ice that is his heart and his own tears that wash the icicle from his eye – once again, a happy ending!

*   *   *

THE SNOW QUEEN

KAY: Those are lovely roses Grandma, it's surprising to see them growing so late, it's almost Winter. I think I saw some flakes of snow earlier. They looked like a swarm of white bees. I wondered if they had a Queen Bee up there in those dark clouds. I think that at midnight she flies through the streets and looks in at the windows and that's when the ice freezes into those strange patterns. Will you tell us some more of those lovely stories while we have our hot milk tonight? Gerda, come over here, Grandma is going to tell us some more stories. I'll just shut the window so that we stay warm and cosy. I was right! It has started to snow – look, there's one huge snowflake there, it's, it's ….it looks like a woman in a beautiful white dress of shining, glittering ice. She's looking at me. If that's the Snow Queen she's not coming in here – I will make her sit on the stove and then she'll melt away! Ow! Something has struck me here (*He puts his hand over his heart)* It was nothing, it must have been something the wind blew in. Oh! I've got something in my eye. Don't worry, I think it's gone. Go away Gerda and stop fussing you stupid little girl. Oh, don't cry, you look even uglier when you cry and you sound like a squeaking cat. No Grandma, I don't need your help. I don't need anyone's help. You are too old and feeble to help me anyway

Look at these roses, I didn't notice that before, they're all worm eaten and horrible. I'll throw them out, and this awful vase. So? It's an heirloom? Who cares about that. There's no room for sentimentality these days.*(He takes the roses and the vase and throws it out through the door)* Good riddance. I'm going to play with my soldiers. I'll make them fight each other and kill each other, that will be fun. No, I don't want to listen to any of those stupid stories, they're just for babies. Gerda can listen if she likes, because she's a baby, a cry baby, an ugly cry baby. No Grandmother, I won't listen. Have you seen how silly you look when you tell those stories *(He begins to mimic her)* Now tonight children I'm going to tell you a story about a Princess and a handsome Prince. They lived happily ever after. *(As himself)* How stupid is that? Nobody lives happily ever after. I'm going to go out and play on my sledge, it'll be much more exciting than staying in here with you two. Goodbye. *(He leaves)*.

*   *   *

11

THE LITTLE
MERMAID

✝

66 "The Little Mermaid" has been immortalised by Walt Disney of course and we all have an image of Ariel in our minds. However, the original story has a touchingly poignant ending for the little mermaid who has yearned to gain her human form can only return to being a mermaid if she kills the Prince with whom she has fallen in love. Unable to do this, she has to watch him marry his earthly Princess and she joins the daughters of air to work for three hundred years to obtain an immortal soul. If you've only seen the film, do try to read this wonderful story. In this scene, however, it is one of the little mermaid's older sisters who is speaking and relating the excitement and wonder of what she saw when she went up to the surface of the water.

*   *   *

THE LITTLE MERMAID

MERMAID PRINCESS: My sisters! Oh my sisters, come here quickly. I have so much to tell you! I saw such amazing things when I went up to the surface of the water. Do you remember Pearl, when you went up and you told us about the lights of the town twinkling like a hundred stars? And the music and the bells and the clatter of the carriages? Well I heard much more than that. Then when you went up Anemone you said you saw the gold and rosy coloured sky and the violet clouds and the flock of swans flying into the sunset? Well I saw much more than that. I did! You two only saw the evening and the night, but I went up for a whole day. Did you know that there are rivers that cross the land and flow down into the sea? No, of course you don't – well I swam up one. It was hard work because the water was trying to go in the other direction, but as I'm such a good swimmer I managed it. It would have been a bit hard for you Foam, but I saw soft hills with lovely outbursts of green coral that they called trees. In the trees there were birds and they were singing! They were singing just as sweetly as I sing and a lot sweeter than you sing Shell ! I listened to them for such a long time. The sky was blue and the sun was so hot that I had to keep diving under the water to stay cool. Look, I think it made my skin turn pink. Come closer – you won't believe what I saw next. There were little human children running in and out of the water and they were swimming and splashing about and they had no tails. I'm not making it up. Oh, Grandmother, tell them it's true, tell them that humans don't have tails. And there was this great fierce animal with black fur and shining eyes and it came right up to me and sniffed at me like this *(she sniffs)* and then it made such a frightening noise that I had to go down deep and find a place to hide. It had sharp teeth and a long tongue. I thought it was going to eat me. When it ran out of the water it shook its fur and all the drops of water went everywhere. No, it didn't have a tail like us, it just had a funny sort of waving thing on its back. Well if you don't believe me you can go up and look for yourselves. Anyway, I just want to get these flowers out of my hair and these oysters off my tail now, they pinch. Yes grandmother, I know they show my rank, but that black monster didn't seem to care about my rank, or the children swimming in the river. Quite frankly, I'm glad to be back down here. Whose turn is it next?

*   *   *

12

THE
NIGHTINGALE

✝

I think this story by Hans Anderson has great relevance today in this age of automation, so many new gadgets and the philosophy of discarding anything that has outlived its transient use. That is why I've given the character of this mechanical nightingale a contemporary feel. In the story, the Emperor turns from the real nightingale to the novelty of the all singing, all dancing clockwork one until, of course, it breaks down and is simply discarded. Perhaps if he had had a computer chip the story would have been very different!

*   *   *

THE NIGHTINGALE

THE MECHANICAL NIGHTINGALE: *(Trying to move his wings)* Twee…Twee… Oh dear, that spring's really gone now. My voice is very croaky too. Well they didn't look after me did they. I need a bit of oil every now and then, that's not too much to ask is it and if they wind that key up too tight my springs just snap. Ooh! I quiver just thinking about it. So, here I am, thrown in the corner with all the rest of you and left to go rusty. I was so beautiful once, all covered in rubies and emeralds and diamonds. I twinkled brighter than Shangai on a Saturday night. I remember the night the Emperor saw me for the first time – dazzled he was, and everybody in the court they gasped – just like this. *(she gasps)* "Eat you heart out Faberge and your flipping eggs" I said to myself. I knew I'd made a bit of an impression. I'll be on to a good thing here, I thought. This could see me through to a comfy retirement, even a bit of publicity you know – Hello magazine, television appearances, maybe even a background role in the next James Bond film. Or Harry Potter. Those owls aren't much use are they. They'd be much better off with a lovely mechanical bird like me. They could programme me to warn them when Voldemort was around. Oh yes, I had it all planned. I was quite happy to twitter away on my perch for them and twirl around a bit. I could only do waltzes, but we've all got our limitations haven't we. I mean Maria Callas was never top of the pops was she? Anyway, the chap who made me made a few bob I can tell you. They even gave him a title – "Imperial

Nightingale Bringer in Chief". There was no stopping him after that, he started making mechanical dogs and cats and even a mechanical mouse, but they all started chasing each other round the Palace and the Emperor wasn't too happy about that. Of course, if he'd been up to date and knew a bit about computers he could have given me a chip and I could have been remote control, then they wouldn't have needed a key and the Emperor could have sat on his throne and switched me on and off to his heart's content. I just went you see. There I was, singing away and I must have moved a bit awkwardly and crack, I heard it go. There was a whirr and a ping and I couldn't move a thing. They got a watchmaker in to look at me, but he didn't have a clue. I mean, watches are digital nowadays aren't they and all he asked was "Where's the battery?" So here I am, in the junk cupboard, and they've had to go out and get the real thing again. I ask you, what can a real nightingale do that I can't. Fly? Oh yes, you've got a point there. Oh well.

*   *   *

13

THE
RED SHOES

✝

There's something about red shoes that has a great appeal for storytellers – after all, Dorothy walked to the Emerald City in the ruby slippers. In this story by Hans Anderson, however, the red shoes have a much more sinister effect on the wearer. Karen, the wearer of the shoes finds that she cannot take them off and has to continue dancing while the shoes still exert their power. She gets so desperate that she asks someone to cut off her feet and finally she dies, so this is one story that doesn't have a happy ending – or does it? For the last lines of the story say:

"Her soul flew on sunbeams to Heaven and no-one was there who asked after the red shoes!"

*   *   *

THE RED SHOES

KAREN: Oh the Princess was so beautiful! And her shoes were red. The finest Morrocan leather and so soft. Did you see them? No, I know your eyesight isn't too good now, but those shoes were so bright. Can I have shoes like that? Please? Yes, I know that red shoes aren't really suitable for a confirmation, but I had a pair once and you threw them away. They were the first shoes I had ever had and I loved them very much. Oh very well, I'll have a look at what the shoemaker has to offer. *(she enters the shop)* Good-day sir, I need some new shoes for my confirmation, may I see what you have. *(To the old lady)*Yes, there are lots of lovely shoes here. I'll try some on and tell you what they look like. *(She walks along the line of shoes)* Oh! You have a pair of r... beautiful shoes. Made for a Count's daughter? I suppose that must be why they are so lovely. Why on earth didn't she take them? They didn't fit her! Then perhaps they will fit me, can I try them? *(She sits and tries on the shoes)* They feel like soft gloves and they fit me perfectly. *(To the old lady)* Can you see the shoes? No, it's a bit dark in here. Yes, they are of beautiful leather. Yes, they shine, oh how they shine; may I have them? Oh thank you. I feel as if they were made just for me. They are the most beautiful shoes in the whole world. Can I wear them home? Come on, I can't wait to show everyone my new shoes.*(She leaves the shop)* Oh dear, it's very muddy out here, I hope it doesn't spoil my shoes. *(She sees the old soldier)* Who are you and what do you want? Go away, for we have to get to church for my confirmation this evening. Oh very well, you can wipe the mud from my shoes because they are new and I love them more than anything in the world. But be very careful for they were made for a Count's daughter and now they're mine. Dancing shoes? No. They're not dancing shoes. I can't dance. Oh, what's happening to me? *(She dances a few steps)* My feet won't go where I want them to go, and my legs won't keep still. It's as though the shoes are making them dance. *(She does a few more steps.)* Stop! I can't stop! I must take the shoes off or I'll never stop. *(She sits down and tries to take off the shoes)* They won't come off. These shoes won't come off my feet.

*   *   *

14

CINDERELLA

✝

"Cinderella" is the classic rags to ritches story that warms the heart of any young girl who yearns to meet her handsome prince. The original story has some really dark moments in it however and the most gruesome part is when the Ugly Sisters start chopping off their toes and heels to get their feet into the glass slipper. Of course, the fairy godmother always seems to be all sweetness and light, but I wondered how tedious that job might be when things didn't go right and you were a less than young and patient godmother!

*   *   *

CINDERELLA

THE FAIRY GODMOTHER: Right, that's it! I have had it with this fairy godmother stuff. Just because I made Sleeping Beauty sleep for 100 years they've given me this job. I saved her life didn't I? And she looked just as good when she woke up. Her dress was out of fashion I know and there was a bit of gardening to do around the Palace, but the Prince came to the rescue and she lived happily ever after. And now where am I? Trying to make sure that Cinderella tries on that wretched shoe. What did I say to her? You must be back before midnight dear or it will all go wrong. And did she listen? Of course she didn't. She flirted with the Prince, fluttering her eyelashes behind her fan until the very last moment and then made the fatal mistake of dropping her glass slipper on the Palace staircase as the clock was chiming twelve. Clumsy girl. Now he's looking everywhere for her. I should have known. Do you know, when I found her sitting in those ashes looking so scruffy and crying because she couldn't go to the ball, I should have known I was on to a loser. And after all I've done for her she's back there in that kitchen letting those ghastly ugly sisters walk all over her. Well, they won't walk very well at the moment because they've chopped their toes off to try to fit into the shoe. I think the Prince would have a very nasty shock if he found himself having to marry one of them! They are ugly enough when they've made an effort to dress up – can you imagine what it would be like waking up to one of them?! Hear them squeal – "It fits! It fits!" How

60

ridiculous. So, does she come back to me? Does she ask me to help her again? No she does not. She lurks in the shadows there with those scruffy little mice that I had to use to draw her golden coach. So, I'm going to leave her to get herself out of this mess and if she and the Prince finally get together and live happily ever after then I'm the Wicked Witch of the West. Wait a minute – the Wicked Witch of the West, that would be a better job for me so that I wouldn't have to go on helping these goody goodies any more. Yes, that's the job I'll try for next. The Wicked Witch of the West. Bring it on!

*　　*　　*

15

THE
THREE LITTLE
PIGS

✝

Three always seems to be a significant number in fairy stories – there are the three Billy Goats Gruff, the three Bears and the three Little Pigs. In this scene the classic Big Bad Wolf who always gets such a bad press is seen to have reformed. I rather like him now!

*   *   *

THE THREE LITTLE PIGS

THE BIG BAD WOLF: Hey man! Don't look so worried. I ain't going to gobble up any little girls, little pigs, chickens, boys called Peter or anything else really meaty any more. Chill out. Don't look so scared. I've gone veggie. Yeah, you heard me dude. No more meat. So if you're a bean, a carrot or a big green cabbage you better start quaking man. Ha ha ha, you ever seen a quaking cabbage? Well, that old Troll that lived under that bridge was the nearest I ever saw to that, especially when those prissy little goats kept trip trapping over him. That sure made him mad and boy did he go green and quake. But I always kept my cool. Sometimes difficult when you're heading straight for a pot of boiling water, but I had my reputation to think of. Yeah, I was legend in stories, I know, I know.

"Oh Grandma what big teeth you've got"

"All the better to gobble you up". Smirk, grin, salivate. I was told that Anthony Hopkins based his Hannibal Lecter on that.

Sure I was a good actor. "Little Pig, Little Pig, may I come in?" sweet simpering voice; appealing tilt of the head. Thought about trying to get on TV or Hollywood. But everytime I bared these fangs everybody ran a mile. I was having a personality crisis man.

"Oh no, it's the big Bad Wolf!" they'd all shriek and run away. I mean, look at me. I ain't big – not big like an elephant or a whale. And if Jaws can become an overnight star then why not me? Even as wolves go I'm neat – and sweet. Not a bad bone in my body. It was all an act. The Big Bad bit is my alter ago. It was peer pressure that made me go ahead and do all that gobbling up and things.

"You're a wolf so you gotta be mean and bad" they kept telling me. And then I got a bad press. So now that's all changed. I'm into peace and love man, no growling, no howling, no lurking with intent and definitely no gobbling. Ban the bomb, save the whale, look at your carbon footprint and think about global warming and brotherly love. And eat lettuce. Lettuce....*(There is a telling grimace)* Yeah, I'm a reformed character kids – and you'd better believe that.

*   *   *

16

THE THREE BEARS

✝

So from The Three Little Pigs to The Three Bears, a story that has entertained children for many generations. It always intrigued me to know what happened afterwards. Where did Goldilocks go and what did the bears do once she had gone? In this age of everyone wanting compensation for anything unfortunate that happens to them their reactions might have a more amusing twist.

*   *   *

THE THREE BEARS

MOTHER BEAR: *(Sitting on a deckchair or sunlounger)* So I said to her – "Listen darling, you can't come breaking into someone's house, eating their porridge, smashing up their furniture and squatting in their beds and expect to get away with it scot free". She didn't have much colour before, but she went very pale at that.

"Please don't call the police", she begged. Yes, she was begging. "Please just let me go home. I won't do anything like this again. Mummy and Daddy would be ever so cross if it got into the papers. They wouldn't be able to go to the golf club until it had all blown over and Mummy would have to put her bridge parties on hold. They wouldn't give me an asbo would they?" She was really quaking now.

"They might, if we pressed charges", I said, as the penny began to drop. "So Daddy plays golf and Mummy plays bridge".

"Yes. And Mummy and I go riding and Daddy plays polo."

"And I expect you've got a big house and several four wheel drives…."

"And a convertible"

"And a convertible and a gardener and a nanny." She nodded.

"So what's a wealthy young lady like you doing stealing other people's porridge?" I asked her. "Doesn't your mother make you any?"

"No. She can't cook. I'm sorry, I was just hungry and it smelt so good."

She was beginning to cry now and to tell you truth I was feeling a bit sorry for her. She was quite a sweet little thing. But I knew I had to stick to my guns. "And do you realise how traumatised Baby Bear is?" I said, "I'm thinking of calling my solicitor and getting him to sue for compensation for mental anguish to a small bear. It could take him years to recover. That was his favourite chair and he's scared to go upstairs now. How would you feel if you found someone sleeping in your bed? And he can't bring himself to eat porridge any more. Too many memories. The claim could run into millions. Your Dad would soon be selling his golf clubs and his convertible."

Well, to cut a long story short, we didn't have to get a solicitor. And we're really enjoying this cruise. All round the Greek islands we've been. I could get used to a life a luxury.

*   *   *

17

LUCKY PEER

✝

The story of "Lucky Peer" is a very long one and tells the life history of a young boy who, although born into a family of moderate means, always nurtures a passionate ideal to be a performer of some sort. He does eventually become a composer and writes a wonderful opera, only to die on its opening night! His first experience of a theatre is given to him by his Godfather who takes him, as a young lad, to the theatre where he is working behind the scenes. There is a ballet called "Samson" being performed and the young Peer is entranced. He tells his mother about it when he returns home. I like his genuine sense of wonderment, something I think we have all experienced on our first visit to a real theatre.

* * *

LUCKY PEER

PEER: Mother! Grandmother! I have had such a wonderful evening! Godfather put me in a special place where I could see the whole show. It was a ballet about a very strong man called Samson. Before it started there was a flood of light and right at the front, coming up out of the earth were all these musicians with flutes and violins, then suddenly everything became quiet. A man dressed in black waved a little black fairy wand over the musicians – like this – and then they began to play and their music filled the whole theatre. I thought that this was all that was going to happen, but then, and you won't believe this, the wall that was at the front that had angels and clouds and things painted on it suddenly rose, as if God himself was pulling it up to Heaven and there was a garden, full of beautiful flowers. The sun was shining but I couldn't see where from and people danced and leapt around the stage – like this! *(He demonstrates)* Yes, yes I will be careful of the ornaments. It was a more wonderful sight than I could ever have imagined. But then there came different scenes. There were soldiers marching and the music was really strong and then a banquet with a huge table and the mighty Samson and his lover sat there. Of course I know she was his lover, Godfather told me. But she was as wicked as she was beautiful, and she betrayed him. She cut his hair – like this – while he was asleep and he lost all his strength because you see, his strength was in his hair! It was! Then the Philistines took him away and made him blind and forced him to work in a mill where they mocked him and laughed at him. That was a very sad scene, but after the break they decided to bring him back to the banquet hall where everyone could laugh at him. But guess what had happened? Go on, guess. His hair had grown and all his strength had come back so when they put him between these two HUGE pillars that must have been real stone, he put his hands on them – like this – and pushed and pushed and pushed and pushed with all his might. Then there were all sorts of flames of green and red and flashes and dust and smoke and the whole place came falling down with a great crash of cymbals and drums and everyone screaming and rushing round all over the stage.I thought the whole theatre might collapse, but it didn't. It was wonderful. I could have gone on watching it all night. Afterwards as Godfather and I walked through the back of the stage we saw knights in gold helmets and angels with wings and beautiful maidens in gauzy dresses – I thought I was in Heaven. Bed?! How can I go to bed when I've just been to the theatre!

*   *   *

18

THE BEETLE WHO WENT ON HIS TRAVELS

✝

"The Beetle Who Went on His Travels" isn't a very well known story by Hans Anderson, but I think we might all know someone like the Beetle who always thinks that they deserve more than they will ever get! Originally the beetle, who lived with the Emperor's horse in his stable, craved a pair of gold shoes just like the horse, and when he couldn't get them he decided to go out into the world to seek his fortune, but he was rather glad to get back to where he started in the end! In these days when reality TV is so popular, he might be an ideal candidate for one of these programmes.

*   *   *

THE BEETLE WHO WENT ON HIS TRAVELS

BEETLE: Good afternoon. You've made absolutely the right decision to see me today and I know I'll be an ideal contestant on your reality travel show, because I am indeed a great traveller. Believe me, I have seen the world! China? Well, no, I haven't actually been to China, but I've been IN some china. You see I was talking to some very stupid frogs, who had a penchant for lying in cold, wet ditches. "Have you ever been to the Emperor's stable?" I asked them, "Where the moisture is warm and refreshing", but they didn't reply, and I never ask a question twice, so I went on my way, stumbling against a piece of broken crockery, which certainly didn't ought to have been there, but you know how careless and untidy humans are. Anyway, as it happened it turned out to be the home of several families of earwigs - never a creature that I could say I've warmed to, I think it's those pincers. But anyway, I had a lucky escape there because the mother had her eye on me as a son-in-law. I was out of there pretty quickly I can tell you! What's that? Have I been to Brussels? No alas, but I once had to sail across a ditch on the leaf of a brussel sprout. I thought I'd get to the other side and be off again, but how wrong I was. Two objectionable little boys came and carried me home to add to their specimens. I considered this a great insult I can tell you so as soon as my wings were dry I hot winged it as fast as I could. They were all set to tie me up and that's the last thing you want, to TAIWAN up! That's a joke, and I haven't been there either. Anywhere else? Delaware? Well I don't know about her, but let me tell you I found myself wearing some horrible damp linen once after being washed onto someone's lawn in a rainstorm. Very unpleasant I can tell you. Put me in a very bad temper. The ladybirds were all flitting about twittering, "Isn't it lovely here?" and the fat caterpillar smirked and remarked how beautiful it was. "Do you call this beautiful?" I said. "I'm accustomed to much better things, there isn't a dunghill anywhere in sight." No, I haven't been in a pan either, sorry Japan, but I've been in a shoe....What's that? I haven't got enough experience? You must be joking! Well, it's your loss. I believe they're looking for something different on the X Factor - and I've certainly got that!

*   *   *

19

THE GIRL WHO
TROD ON A LOAF

✝

Here's another story by Hans Anderson that is probably new to you. In "The Girl who trod on the Loaf", a really obnoxious little girl called Inge eventually learns what it is like to be on the wrong side of nastiness like hers. When she treads on a loaf to avoid getting her shoes wet crossing a marsh, she is sucked down into another world and is taught a lesson! It has echoes of "A Christmas Carol" I think and I know how popular to act are Roald Dahl's ghastly children, so here's another one!

*   *   *

THE GIRL WHO TROD ON THE LOAF

INGE: I won't! I won't come in yet. I haven't caught enough flies yet. Come here you pathetic little flapping, flitting fly, I want to pull your wings off. See how I'll do it. Just like that. And then you'll have to crawl around in the mud. *(She laughs)* I love watching you struggle. It's like that boy in the village when he fell into the pond and couldn't swim. I laughed my head off. Last week I caught a beetle and I stuck his feet onto a leaf and watched him trying to escape. When I turned him upside down he looked as if he was trying to turn the pages of a book. Of course beetles can't read - can they? I wonder what a beetle would read if it could. "The handbook for rescuing flies from mud" maybe. I thought he ought to turn over a new leaf! Oh, I'm so funny I make myself laugh. My mother tells me I need to turn over a new leaf. "Inge", she says, "Your headstrong will requires severity to conquer it", whatever that means. I don't know anybody called Headstrong Will, unless he's related to Bill - that's Bill Stickers and he's always being prosecuted! *(More laughter)* Oh, I should have been a comedian. And then she goes on, "Now you just tread upon my apron, but soon you will tread upon my heart". I ask you. Is that going over the top or what. Mothers, I don't know why they don't just chill out. She says she's going to send me to rich family in the village who will teach me manners and how to dress properly. Like ladette to lady isn't it. Well I don't want them to put me in any fancy gear like frocks and stuff. How can you go out and catch flies and beetles in a frock?! I expect they'll want me to brush my hair and put bows in it too and take off my boots and wear pretty little shoes. And what about my reputation? I'm known for being the hardest girl in the village. When other kids see me coming they run. Oh boy do they run, because they know that if I catch them, they'll be just like those flies and beetles. So I won't go in and I won't go to this stupid family and I won't listen to my mother. Just try and make me.

*   *   *

20

THE BRAVE
LITTLE TAILOR

✝

The stories of the Brothers Grimm are often quite dark and violent, but the story of "The Brave Little Tailor" does have a happy ending, despite quite a lot of fighting and killing on the way. I can't help wondering, however, whether his marriage to the Princess would go on being happy once she had discovered who he really was. In today's society where newspapers, magazines and television journalists all seem obsessed by the private lives of the famous, they might get more exposure than they want!

*   *   *

THE BRAVE LITTLE TAILOR

REPORTER: Look Bill, I'm telling you, this story is huge! I'm outside the palace now and there's so much coming and going it's like Grand Central Station. I managed to grab a few of the servants as they were coming off the night shift and although it took a bit of bribery, I managed to corroborate the story that she hired a couple of hoodlums to come in in the dead of night and ship him off somewhere, then they reckoned she'd spread the story that he'd disappeared. I wouldn't be surprised if her father was behind it mind you because I don't think he ever imagined he'd complete all those awesome tasks and he'd have to keep his promise and give him half the kingdom and his daughter. I mean, how stupid is that? Someone you've only just met tells you they're a great hero and you believe them. Did he look him up on You Tube? I think not? Did he check his criminal record? No he didn't. Well yes, he did do all those tasks, getting rid of the giants and the unicorn and the boar, but does that make him the right person to be king? Of course the anti monarchy lobby is out in force and they were only too keen to share their views. I quote: "We spend our money on keeping these people in an archaic situation of privilege and they turn out to be no better than common criminals." Strong words Bill, strong words and I don't know that I agree with them, but if he does turn out to be nothing more than a common little tailor then that rubbishes their argument and good luck to him I say. Hello, there's more activity now. I think it's the Princess's car. She hasn't been seen in public or made any statement yet and what we've heard has just been speculation. Is he with her I wonder? No, she seems to be on her own. *(Rushing over to the car)* Princess! Princess! Is it true that you and your husband are splitting up? Can you give us a statement Princess? No, she didn't give any indication of what's going on. What's that Bill? He is? Now? OK. Live on air in two. How do I look? Yeah I know I've been up all night but at least tell me I don't look like it. 5-4-3-2=1 Good morning . This is Charlie Humdinger live at the palace bringing you all the latest on the sensational news story that has just broken. I understand we are about to go over to the palace library where his majesty the King will make a statement….

*   *   *

Other books by this author from CheckPoint Press
ISBN: 978-1-906628-23-9 Poems for Children to Enjoy
ISBN: 978-1-906628-19-2 More Poems for Children to Enjoy
ISBN: 978-1-906628-46-8 Scenes for Young Performers to Enjoy (II)

CheckPoint Press
Books for Training and Education

www.checkpointpress.com

Lightning Source UK Ltd.
Milton Keynes UK
UKOW04f0802270415

250397UK00001B/14/P